IMAGES
of America

CAMPBELL

PICTURESQUE. Orchard Valley is in bloom in this 1929 photograph taken by E. Standish.

IMAGES
of America

CAMPBELL

Campbell Historical Museum & Ainsley House
Karen Brey

ARCADIA
PUBLISHING

Published by Arcadia Publishing
Charleston SC, Chicago IL, Portsmouth NH, San Francisco CA

Library of Congress Catalog Card Number: 2004107078

For all general information, contact Arcadia Publishing:
Telephone 843-853-2070
Fax 843-853-0044
E-mail sales@arcadiapublishing.com
For customer service and orders:
Toll-free 1-888-313-2665

Visit us on the Internet at www.arcadiapublishing.com

SPREADING FRUIT. Workers of Geo. E. Hyde & Co. spread fruit for the drying yard.

CONTENTS

ACKNOWLEDGMENTS

The Campbell Historical Museum & Ainsley House is proud to present this pictorial history of Campbell. The book would not have been possible without the previous research of Jeanette Watson. From a ·longtime Campbell family, Jeanette was the driving force for the museum's establishment in 1964 and served as its early volunteer curator. Her book *Campbell, the Orchard City* provided the basis for this book. Special kudos to author and museum curator Karen Brey for compiling the images from the collection of the Campbell Historical Museum & Ainsley House, developing the thematic chapters, and weaving the history into both the introduction and captions to best tell our story.

The museum is grateful to the hundreds of people who have donated photographs, scrapbooks, and archival materials to our collection over the years. Because of their generosity we are able to tell the story of this area and reflect on how people lived in times past. Preservation of Campbell's history and the surrounding area is the most significant part of our mission. We would be remiss if we did not pay homage to the Country Woman's Club in Campbell, which in 2005 celebrates its 100-year anniversary and which founded the museum, providing space and nourishment before turning its collection over to the City of Campbell to maintain.

Finally, thanks go to the City of Campbell for its support of the museum and to the community itself for recognizing the importance of preserving local history and the stories that are important for future generations to have and to remember.

The museum would also like to acknowledge Arcadia Publishing and editor Hannah Clayborn for their support and encouragement, making the publication of this book possible. We are delighted to be a part of Arcadia's Images of America series.

—Gloria Chun Hoo, Director
Campbell Historical Museum & Ainsley House

INTRODUCTION

The landscape of our rich Santa Clara Valley has undergone dramatic changes over the past 200 years. For centuries the Ohlone lived in the rich grass- and oak-filled valley. Fishing in the numerous streams, hunting the abundant wildlife, and gathering acorns from the thousands of oak trees, the Ohlone lived in seasonal villages.

The Ohlone way of life was changed forever with the founding of Mission Santa Clara de Asis and the Pueblo de San Jose de Guadalupe in 1777 by the Spanish. The Spanish padres used the local Ohlone to plant fields of wheat to sustain the vast herds of cattle that grazed the valley floor. When Mexico won independence from Spain in 1821, the land was divided into vast ranchos, and cattle roamed freely throughout the valley. By petitioning the Mexican government, one could obtain up to 50,000 acres of land. As the Spanish before them, the "Californios" utilized the land mainly for raising livestock. With the discovery of gold in 1848 and the coming of statehood, many newcomers began migrating to the fertile Santa Clara Valley.

In 1851, five years after arriving in California, Benjamin Campbell purchased 160 acres of former Mission grazing land. He then traveled back east to Missouri to marry his sweetheart, Mary Louise Rucker. Benjamin Campbell led a wagon train of 43 adults and children back to Campbell, California. The Campbells, like many others, soon built a farmhouse and began growing wheat. Their treelined driveway to the Campbell ranch house is now Campbell Avenue.

In the 1870s, as fruit orchards sprung up throughout the valley, the Campbells and other ranchers granted the South Pacific Coast Railroad a right of way through their land to help transport crops to outside markets. Soon roads were built to connect neighbors to the railroad line, and the Campbell home became the area's first post office. In 1886, with the building of a small depot called "Campbell Station," the town became a hub of activity. In 1888, Ben and Mary Campbell started to subdivide their land, which eventually became downtown Campbell.

The completion of the transcontinental railroad in 1869 allowed Santa Clara Valley farmers to open up the agricultural market to consumers back east. Fruit orchards and small family farms became a way of life in the valley. Campbell became known as the "Orchard City." Its economy and population began to develop around the thriving food-growing industry.

As early as 1887, many local orchardists began to pool their crops to sell to packers in Campbell and the Santa Clara Valley. By banding together in cooperatives, farmers found they could weather the ups and downs of a fickle economy. In 1892, the Campbell Fruit Growers Union formed, adopting its trademark of a comical two-humped camel. Grower-owned companies and cooperatives became the industry standard. By 1917, Campbell's two main cooperatives, the Campbell Fruit Growers Union and the Campbell Farmers Union Packing Company, were absorbed into the statewide California Prune and Apricot Growers Union (which was widely known as Sunsweet).

Vast improvements in commercial canning methods occurred during the 1890s, led by pioneers such as John Colpitts Ainsley of Campbell. The town was becoming renowned for its fruit products and some of the finest canneries in California. By 1900, the advent of new canning machinery was making mass production a reality. While family-run orchards still surrounded the town, canneries and drying yards provided work for hundreds of people, creating an economy that helped the tiny town grow and develop. Perley Payne Sr. started his Orchard City Canning Co., winning a Bronze Medal at the 1915 Panama Pacific Exposition in San Francisco for its excellent product. At the peak of the 1929 season, the J.C. Ainsley Packing Co. employed about 750 people, and the Geo. E. Hyde & Co. cannery expanded into its "modern" facilities; its large brick buildings house offices today.

In 1952, the City of Campbell finally voted for incorporation. The fire station, built at 51 North Campbell Avenue, became the first building owned by the new city. From 1952 to 1957, the building served as the fire station, police station, and city offices. The fire engines occupied the front of the building, and the police and city clerk shared an office. The city clerk, Dorothy Trevethan, had three phones on her desk: one for the fire department, one for the police department, and one for city business. Now the old fire station is the location of the Campbell Historical Museum. J.C. Ainsley's 1925 home, originally on 88 acres, was moved in 1990 to downtown historic Campbell and today is a historic house museum. Campbell's former high school is now a historic landmark that has been converted to house the city's community center and Heritage Theatre. The historic downtown, although still only four blocks long, continues to thrive with many shops and restaurants.

Today, Campbell proudly retains its small-town identity. The valley orchards have given way to highways, homes, and high-tech industries. Through all of these changes, the people of this valley—their energy, creativity, and industry—continue to make Campbell a part of the "Valley of Heart's Delight."

BENJAMIN CAMPBELL. This picture shows the man for whom the City of Campbell is named.

One

EARLY CAMPBELL

GEO. E. HYDE & CO. This label for Sun-Tint Brand Sliced Yellow Cling Peaches is from 1920. (Courtesy of Bernard M. Strojny, City Manager.)

BENJAMIN AND MARY RUCKER CAMPBELL, 1851. Benjamin Campbell, founder of the town that bears his name, came to California with his father, William, in 1846. In 1851, Benjamin returned to Missouri to marry his sweetheart, Mary Rucker. The couple is shown here in their wedding portrait. Campbell then led a wagon train of 43 people back to California.

BENJAMIN CAMPBELL'S THRESHING MACHINE. In 1851, this wheat-threshing machine was the only one of its kind in the Santa Clara Valley. The Campbells hired the machine out after threshing their fields. The Campbells threshed up to 300 bushels a day in July and bragged to relatives in Illinois that it was the only good threshing machine in California.

BENJAMIN CAMPBELL'S RANCH. This image from the 1876 *Atlas of Santa Clara County* shows where Benjamin and Mary bought 160 acres of former Mission grazing land, built a farmhouse, and began growing wheat. Later the Campbells subdivided their land, which eventually became the City of Campbell. Present-day Campbell Avenue is the driveway that runs up to the house.

(LEFT) **BENJAMIN AND MARY CAMPBELL'S DAUGHTERS.** Pictured are, from left to right, Laura Ann (1854–1895) and Lena Malicia (1856–1930).

(RIGHT) **JAMES AND JESSIE CAMPBELL.** James Henry Campbell, Ben and Mary's only son, and Jessie McKenzie pose for their wedding portrait in December 1895.

THE FIRST HOME OF BENJAMIN AND MARY CAMPBELL, 1883. Ben Campbell (age 52) is in the foreground on the right with his son-in-law William Swope behind him. Ben's daughter Lena and her husband, Samuel George Rodeck, are sitting on the porch. Other members of the Campbell family are around the house.

12

CAMPBELL FRIENDS AND FAMILY, 1898. The Campbells' friends and family pose for Benjamin Campbell's 72nd birthday celebration in 1898. Benjamin Campbell, with a beard, is seated in the center behind the railing. His wife, Mary Campbell, stands behind him in the printed dress.

RUCKER FAMILY PORTRAIT. In 1851, Benjamin Campbell made his second trip to California after he was married in Missouri. He led eight covered wagons containing family members, including the Campbells, the Finleys (his sister's family), and the Ruckers (his wife's family), on the overland trail.

BENJAMIN AND MARY CAMPBELL'S SECOND HOME. The Campbells' second home was located on Campbell Avenue and First Street. The Campbells are in the surrey. The windmill and tank house were functioning necessities of the ranch.

THE SWOPE FAMILY, SEPTEMBER 5, 1894. Benjamin Campbell's daughter Laura married William Swope, and this photograph was taken at their home on Central Avenue. The Swope family members pictured here are, from left to right, Alda Swope Blaine, Ethel Swope Davis, Lena Swope French, William Swope, and Laura Campbell Swope.

LENA SWOPE FRENCH, C. 1905. Lena Swope, Benjamin Campbell's granddaughter, poses for her high school portrait.

15

CAMPBELL DEPOT. In 1877, the Campbells gave the South Pacific Coast Railroad permission to lay tracks through their property. Ben Campbell sold 1.15 acres of land to the railroad in 1886 so it could build a depot with a telegraph office. The depot created an important link to bigger towns, which helped put Campbell on the map.

DOWNTOWN CAMPBELL, C. 1895. This view of Central Avenue shows the first Methodist church on the left and the steeple of the first Congregational church in the middle. The backs of Campbell Hall and Willet's store are on the right.

DOWNTOWN CAMPBELL, 1890S. This photograph of Campbell Avenue was taken from the Ainsley Packing Company water tower. Harrison Avenue (in the foreground) ends at Campbell Avenue, as it does today. The buildings are, from left to right, Lloyd's General Repairs and Horseshoeing, Campbell Hall, and Willet's General Store. On the left, heading south toward Los Gatos, is the Southern Pacific track. In preparation for Ben and Mary Campbell's new subdivision, the Campbell Hall Association was created in 1886. The association built Campbell Hall to be the center of town with room for meetings and social functions.

RURAL FREE DELIVERY CARRIAGE. In 1897, Campbell became the first rural route established in the West. The rural free delivery was established in a few select areas to test the system. Rural mail carriers were mobile post offices that carried stamps and postal cards. Campbell proved to be one of the most successful routes established and helped to prove the viability of rural free delivery. The photograph features one of Campbell's first three rural free delivery carriages.

CHARLES TOWNSEND IN A MAIL-DELIVERY RIG. In 1897, Charles Townsend was appointed a carrier for the rural free delivery route. Patrons were advised that the carrier would not stand around while they wrote out a card. Areas around Campbell were so impressed with the service that they began to bombard their congressmen with requests for similar service. By 1899, there were 14 rural routes in California.

FIRST AUTOMOBILE IN CAMPBELL. Charles Townsend is seated in his Maxwell automobile *c.* 1900.

POST OFFICE INTERIOR, MARCH 1926. The photograph shows the post office interior when it was located on the south side of Campbell Avenue. The man in the apron is E.E. Scorser.

MAXWELL'S POST OFFICE ON CAMPBELL AVENUE. Pictured here are, from left to right, Walter Dowton, Henry Young, Charles Townsend, Onie Putnam, and Lottie Miracle, postmaster. Campbell's automated rural free delivery force is triple-parked in front of the post office in the Curry Building in 1914.

SUNDAY SCHOOL PICNIC AT CONGRESS SPRINGS, APRIL 1915. In the background is the Interurban car. The Interurban, from San Jose to Campbell, was finished in 1904. Many

THE 12-PASSENGER BUS, C. 1920. The bus traveled to Los Gatos, Campbell, and San Jose. The first stage, started in 1916, was owned by Floyd Curtis and later bought by Peerless Stages.

Campbell residents used this line, called the "Short Line," to travel to San Jose or out to Saratoga for picnics. The increased use of autos and bus services put an end to the Interurban in 1932.

DOWNTOWN CAMPBELL, 1911. This photograph, taken from the water towers, illustrates downtown Campbell during the 1911 flood. After a torrential rainstorm dumped over 13 inches of water in a few days, 300 feet of the Los Gatos Creek bulkhead gave way only a mile and a half away from downtown Campbell. The flood of 1911 was not the first or last flood in downtown Campbell, but it was the most documented.

WEEKS MEAT MARKET. This photograph, taken at Railroad and Campbell Avenues in 1911, documents one of many floods in Campbell's history. In 1951, another flooding occurred around the San Tomas Creek area. Proponents of incorporating Campbell argued that incorporated residents would have clout to do something about the continual flooding. After many earlier unsuccessful attempts, the incorporation of Campbell was passed after the 1952 flood.

BOAT RIDE. In this picture, Emory Poston takes Gordon Ainsley for a boat ride on Harrison Avenue, opposite the Ainsley Cannery, during the 1911 flood in Campbell.

FLOOD OF 1911. This photograph of downtown Campbell features the intersection of First Street and Campbell Avenue. The buildings on the left belonged to Jim Burns, the Campbell Library, and Ben Campbell (his tank house). Benjamin Campbell's first house is on the left near the trees.

PAN-PACIFIC EXPOSITION IN SAN FRANCISCO, 1915. Attending the exposition and pictured here with the Liberty Bell in the background are Grace and Lois Bohnett, Joseph Bohnett's daughters.

BICYCLISTS IN FRONT OF THE BOHNETT HOME. Joseph Bohnett came to Campbell from Michigan in 1871. He started as a farm laborer, leased a ranch for a while, and then purchased 50 acres in the Cambrian area in 1889. Bohnett immediately replaced the grain fields with prune, apricot, and cherry trees. Bohnett was a charter member of the Orchard City Grange and a trustee for the Cambrian School District.

Two

BUSINESSES

GEO. E. HYDE & CO. This label for Sunnyside Brand Sliced Yellow Cling Peaches is from 1928.

DOWNTOWN CAMPBELL, C. 1900. This picture showing Campbell Avenue was taken from Central Avenue looking east. The Farley Building, formerly the Bank of Campbell, is the corner building on the left; the Campbell Hotel is on the right. The Bank of Campbell was founded in 1895, and today the Farley Building is the oldest business building in Campbell. This photograph and the next three images provide four views of Campbell Avenue that span a period of over 50 years.

DOWNTOWN CAMPBELL, 1909. A postcard of Campbell Avenue in 1909 looking west shows the B.O. Curry Building, the Methodist church, and several bakeries. Postcards of local points of interest were often made to send to relatives back east.

CAMPBELL AVENUE, 1930s. In this picture, the view looks west.

DOWNTOWN CAMPBELL, 1950s. In this photograph from the 1950s, the B.O. Curry Building still stands, as do Clark's Drugs and Benson's Cleaners; farther down is the Busy Bee cafe. The photograph was taken under the black walnut trees that the Swope family planted.

LOUIS GENASCI, EARLY 1900S. Originally from Italy, the Genascis came to Campbell in 1911. In the picture, Louis stands near the cash register in his store, L. Genasci General Merchandise, which he opened on Campbell Avenue soon after his family's arrival. This was a typical "general store" of its time, selling groceries, feed, hardware, and other dry goods.

HAND IN HAND. Posing for this picture are Mr. and Mrs. Louis Genasci.

THE GENASCI FAMILY. Enjoying the beach in Santa Cruz, the two boys pictured are the Genasci sons, from left to right, Ed and Louis Jr.; Louis Sr. and his wife are in the center.

GENASCI DELIVERY WAGON. Genasci's sons Ed and Louis Jr. worked as delivery boys for the store. Young Ed Genasci is seated at the reins of this delivery wagon. Later, Ed Genasci served as the chief of the Campbell Volunteer Fire Department from 1919 to 1941.

EXTERIOR OF OKIDA GENERAL STORE. To serve the growing Japanese community in the surrounding area, the two Okida brothers operated a general store on Campbell Avenue from 1908 to 1911.

OKIDA GENERAL STORE DURING 1911 FLOOD. Unfortunately, the Okida brothers had to move their store to San Jose after their Campbell store was severely damaged in the 1911 flood.

FARMERS UNION GROCERY STORE, 1915. The Farmers Union advertised groceries, general merchandise, hardware, grain, and feed.

FARMER'S UNION DELIVERY WAGON. In 1894, Charles Willet sold his grocery store on Campbell Avenue (which in 1889 had been the first in Campbell) to the Farmers Union. The delivery wagon is backed up to the Farmers Union Grocery Store. Lester Merrill is the driver on the dray, and Jim Kelly sits as "jumper." The *Interurban Press* office is next door.

JOHN H. BLAINE SR. AND FRANK A. BLAINE. John H. Blaine Sr. (left) was the father of Robert, Frank, John D., and Mary Hurlbert. Blaine was a leader of class meetings (held in Campbell Hall) and invented the three-legged orchard ladder, which made access to the fruit much easier. In 1895, Frank Blaine (right), a photographer, and his brother-in-law Elgin Hurlbert introduced the *Campbell Weekly Visitor*, the first known newspaper in Campbell.

BLAINE'S STORE. In 1914, John D. Blaine, who married Benjamin Campbell's granddaughter Alda Swope, opened his own general store. Blaine's store was on the corner of Campbell and Central Avenues until he sold out his stock in 1926. John Blaine is pictured in the center.

BLAINE DELIVERY TRUCK. Pictured here, from left to right, are Ethan Lanphear (later the first Campbell fire chief), Elgin Hurlbert, George Blaine, and Frank Blaine in a Model T grocery delivery truck in 1917.

B.O. CURRY REAL ESTATE & INSURANCE WAGON AND J.F. WEHMEYER GENERAL REPAIRING/HORSE SHOEING. By 1912, Benjamin O. Curry had become so successful in the real estate business that he started in 1891 that he moved out of his false-front building and constructed the two-story, Mission revival–style Curry Building. Curry was also an orchardist, a realtor, the founder of the Growers National Bank of Campbell, a school trustee, and a founding member of Morning Light Lodge No. 42 of the International Order of Odd Fellows. He is also said to have coined the phrase "the Orchard City."

CAMPBELL LAUNDRY. George W. Barnes owned the Campbell Laundry on Central Avenue in the 1920s and 1930s. Note the early advertising of Campbell Laundry on the truck.

INTERIOR OF THE CAMPBELL LAUNDRY. George W. Barnes stands on the right inside the Campbell Laundry.

GROWERS NATIONAL BANK, 1920. Formed in 1919 by B.O. Curry, the Growers National Bank was originally located in Curry's real estate office. In 1920, Curry constructed this Classical Revival building to house the Growers National Bank. Today, the building still stands on Campbell Avenue as the Campbell Gaslight Theater.

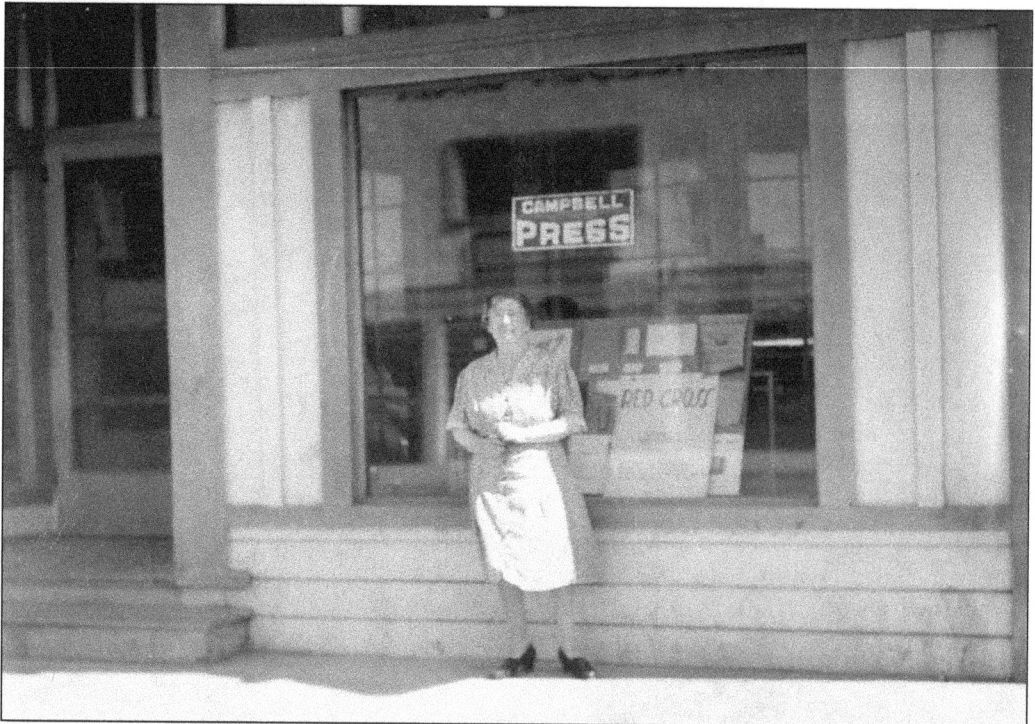

CAMPBELL PRESS. In 1912, Harry and Edna Smith purchased the *Campbell Interurban Press* (later the name was shortened to *Campbell Press*). The Smiths were energetic reporters, editors, and supporters of the community. After Harry's death in 1937, Edna continued the newspaper. This photograph, taken in 1948, shows Edna Fawcett Smith in front of the newspaper office, located on the bottom floor of Campbell Odd Fellows Hall on Campbell Avenue and First Street.

CAMPBELL HOTEL, 1934. The hotel, originally opened as the Sutter Hotel in 1894, was located on the northeast corner of Campbell Avenue and Central Avenue. The two Maxson sisters refurbished and renamed the hotel the Campbell Hotel in 1912. Seven rooms and a bath were upstairs. Downstairs had a two-room apartment, Betty's Beauty Shoppe, a large living and dining room, a kitchen, and a store room. Lunch was served daily at a cost of 35¢.

LUMBERYARD IN CAMPBELL. Photographed are Jim Smith, Mr. French, Jim Conant, and Manuel Conia.

MISSION CHICKEN HATCHERY. Mr. and Mrs. George Ellison were in the hatchery business for many years. In 1916, they built this Mission-style plant on present-day Winchester Boulevard. They could ship up to 25,000 chicks per week, and most of their stock went to Utah and Idaho. Baby chicks are easily shipped because residual yolk material can sustain them for three days.

WINCHESTER HATCHERY. Paul and Frances Oeser opened the Winchester Hatchery in 1937. Also located on Winchester Boulevard, the Winchester Hatchery specialized in heavier breeds for local sale. Paul Oeser originally worked for George Ellison and the Mission Hatchery.

38

WESTERN GRAVEL COMPANY. Around 1940, a group of investors purchased Cunningham & Sons, a small family-owned plant, and formed Western Gravel Company. The gravel operation continued until 1959, when the upstream dams and freeway construction exhausted the local gravel resources.

WESTERN GRAVEL COMPANY. After 1959, the Western Gravel Company expanded into the ready-mixed concrete and general building business until it was sold in 1968. The National Perlite buildings were used for the building materials warehouse after 1952.

BENSON'S CAMPBELL CLEANERS. Lowell and Evelyn Benson owned and operated Benson's Campbell Cleaners from 1938 to 1974. Navy and marine promotional posters are in the front of the building. While her husband served in World War II, Eveyln Benson operated the shop by herself.

SHADLE DRUG STORE. Herbert Shadle opened his pharmacy on Campbell Avenue in 1922.

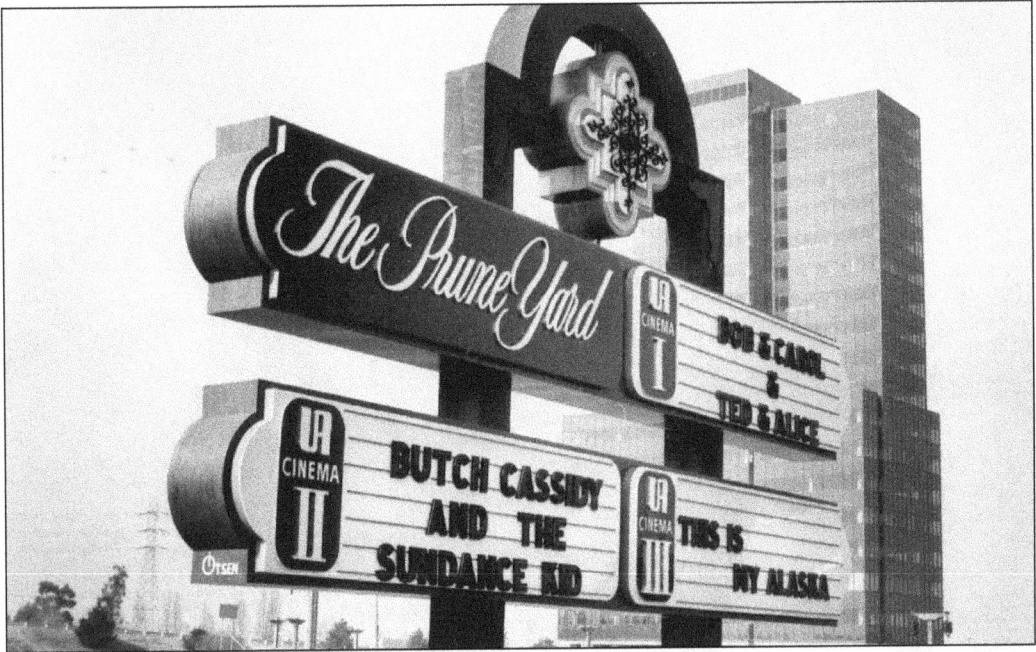

THE PRUNEYARD SHOPPING CENTER, 1970. In 1968, developer Fred Sahadi purchased the Brynteson Ranch to create a mixed-use complex. United Artists Movie Theater was the first business to open its doors in the Pruneyard Shopping Center in 1969. The towers, Campbell's only skyscrapers, are visible in the background.

JOHN BRYNTESON'S CHILDREN. Pictured in the 1920s, from left to right, are Lucile, Ruth, Kermit, Lillie, and Ingleliff. John Brynteson was one of the "lucky Swedes" who struck it rich with Alaskan gold. He came to Campbell and purchased a 60-acre orchard at the intersection of Bascom and Campbell Avenues. The Brynteson ranch remained in the family until 1968.

AERIAL VIEW OF CAMPBELL, 1970. This photograph, taken from the Pruneyard Towers, looks toward Highway 17 and Los Gatos Creek. Today, industrial developments dot the left side of Highway 17, and the Los Gatos Creek trail is on the right.

Three

AGRICULTURE

J.C. AINSLEY PACKING CO. This label for Pansy Brand Apricots is from 1897.

SPRAY RIGS AT QUITO RANCH, C. 1880. In 1846, a Mexican land grant deeded the Saratoga, Cupertino, and Campbell areas to early settlers Jose Noriega and his father-in-law, Jose Fernandez. Later, Manuel Alviso purchased the land grant area and named it Rancho Quito.

GUINCHARD FAMILY ORCHARD, C. 1920. This is a view of the orchard from the San Tomas area, looking from Quito Road east down Pollard Road. Campbell is in the far distance. Apricots, prunes, and other fruit trees first appeared in the Santa Clara Valley during the Mission period. The region's fertile soil and moderate climate encouraged early ranchers to experiment with growing fruit trees. In 1856, immigrants Pierre and Louis Pellier grafted the French prune to the rootstock of the wild plum, creating a prune that was especially suited to the Santa Clara Valley.

MAN PICKING FRUIT. In the picture, a man from Sunsweet picks fruit using a three-legged ladder that John H. Blaine of Campbell invented.

AERIAL VIEW OF CAMPBELL, 1959. Many orchards are still visible in this photograph of downtown Campbell. The water tower that stands today can be seen to the left. The water tower in the center is no longer standing. Campbell experienced a boom in the 1980s along with the rest of Silicon Valley. It was at this time that the last of the orchards in Campbell disappeared.

46

PARR FAMILY, C. 1895. Edward Noah Parr was a farmer who owned over 400 acres near San Tomas. He was also a founding trustee of the Campbell School District. The first classes in the district were held in his granary. Also pictured here at the Edward N. Parr ranch on Sunnyoak Avenue are, from left to right, his wife, Virginia "Jennie" Diana Johnson Parr; Lester Parr; Charles Earl Parr; Edna Lulu Parr; and Hazel Virginia Parr.

ORCHARD IRRIGATION. Campbell was fortunate to have both the Los Gatos Creek and the San Tomas Creek transverse the orchard's boundaries. At one time, the Los Gatos Creek supplied four major irrigation ditch companies. The men pictured with their shovels are probably creating a "check" or levee of dirt about two feet high in order to make use of water from an irrigation ditch.

ORCHARD CITY GRANGE DRILL TEAM, 1907. The Grange began in 1903 as a supportive network for the agricultural community. The group was chartered with 123 members, which was practically everybody in town. The Grange urged the rural free delivery of parcel post and supported organizations like the Farmers Telephone Company. They also had the first drill team in the county.

ORCHARD CITY GRANGE PLANTING REDWOOD TREES, 1927. The Grange was responsible for many of the early beautification projects around Campbell. The Grange also worked on marketing the local fruit crops as well as other local issues such as how to fight "thrip," a small insect.

SCORSUR FARM. In this photograph, Jack Scorsur works the orchard on Union Avenue.

SCORSUR FAMILY, 1900. From left to right, Jack, Andrew, Ellen, Nick, and Nick Jr. pose for a family portrait.

KRKICH ORCHARD, 1926. Two men harvest prunes off the ground at the Krkich ranch. Prunes were left to ripen on the tree and were then picked up off the ground. They were then dipped in a lye solution and laid on trays to dry. Apricots were picked off the tree and cut in half, the pits removed and laid on trays.

KRKICH ORCHARD. Martin Krkich (on the far left) and other men pick apricots in the orchard with wicker wine jugs.

MARTIN KRKICH. In the foreground, Krkich holds his horse behind apricots in a drying tray; the sulfur house is in the back. After the fruit was laid out on trays, it was sulfured and put in the sun to dry. Sulfur was used as a preservative to keep the fruit from rotting before it was laid out in the sun to dry.

KRKICH DRYING YARD, 1920s. It took two men to lift a tray of fruit. The trays were usually stacked shoulder high, and two empty trays were placed on top to shield the fruit from rain. If the fruit became wet, it was ruined.

TAMER BOHNETT WITH CHILDREN, 1902. These children are playing in a prune dipper. This one-person prune dipper was used on small family ranches. Fruit was loaded into a metal basket, dipped in a lye solution, and transferred onto a tray for drying in the yard.

C. ORLANDO AND SONS, 1928. In this photograph, Orlando and his sons are prune dipping and then loading trays onto the wagon to dry in the sunshine.

FRANK DUNCAN'S PRUNE-DRYING SHED, 1880s. Frank Duncan's orchard was located on present-day Bascom Avenue. Frank Duncan also spearheaded the Duncan Ditch Company, a cooperative enterprise that regulated an irrigation stream to each customer.

CHERRY PICKERS. Workers pose for a group photograph on a ranch across Los Gatos Creek, between Casey Road and McGlincy Avenue.

CAMPBELL FRUIT GROWERS UNION, C. 1900. The Fruit Growers Union began in 1892 to join farmers together to help dry, pack, and market their fruit; it was completely grower-owned. The union bought a plant and a dry yard. It was so effective that it was quickly recognized as one of the most important in the valley. Later the union property became the Hyde Cannery.

CAMPBELL FRUIT GROWERS UNION FRUIT SORTERS, C. 1900. These women sort fruit at the Fruit Growers Union's north dryer warehouse.

GOMES FAMILY, 1940S. Joaquin Vincent Gomes arrived in California in the 1880s from Portugal and purchased land in Campbell in 1900. Taking a break from picking prunes on the Gomes ranch are the children of Mr. and Mrs. Joseph V. Gomes (son of Joaquin). Gomes family members pictured here are, from left to right, as follows: (front row) Jeanette Gomes Watson, Joe Gomes Jr., and June Gomes Weitzel; (back row) Rose Furtado (great-aunt of the children), Jerry Gomes, Joyce Gomes, and Jean Gomes.

PETE YERKOVICH AND IDA FURTADO, 1935. Tony Yerkovich, Pete's father, originally came from Yugoslavia and settled an orchard on the corner of Winchester Boulevard and Payne Avenue. The Yerkovich fruit stand was a stopping place for city dwellers for many years. Pete and Ida Yerkovich were longtime volunteers at the Campbell Historical Museum. In this photograph, they pose for their wedding portrait.

YERKOVICH FRUIT STAND, 1950s. The Yerkovich fruit stand was located on Winchester Boulevard. The family operated a 20-acre ranch, with 10 acres in cherries, 4 in apricots, and 6 in prunes. Pictured here are, from left to right, Chester Yerkovich, Jennie Vlasich, Patty Furtado, Jennie Gomes, Antone (Tony) Yerkovich, Jeanette Gomes Watson, June Gomes Weitzel, and Ann Furtado.

Four

CANNERIES AND DRYING YARDS

SUNSWEET CALIFORNIA PRUNES. The date of this label is unknown.

FARMERS UNION PACKING COMPANY, 1912. Organized in 1909, the Campbell Farmers Union Packing Company was a group of growers who felt they could make a cooperative packing and marketing agency work. This is not to be confused with the Farmers Union Grocery Store, which was a separate entity. The union built this packinghouse, the first three-story building in Campbell, in 1912. The first floor was used for packing, the second had bins for fruit storage, and the third contained the grading equipment.

THE FARMERS UNION. This glimpse into the Farmers Union shows workers packing fruit. Farmers created many other organizations similar to the Farmers Union Packing Company throughout the Santa Clara Valley. In 1917, farmers statewide recognized the need for a cooperative to ensure a market for their fruit at realistic prices. The California Prune and Apricot Growers Association emerged and became affiliated with the Campbell Farmers Union Packing Company.

58

INSIDE THE FARMERS UNION PACKING HOUSE. The numbers "70–80" on the bags refer to the number of prunes in a pound. If the prunes were large, the number of prunes per pound would be smaller, and the price would be better. The prunes were shoveled into 100-pound sacks indicating that they were to be shipped to Hamburg, Germany.

JOHN COLPITTS AINSLEY, 1891. J.C. Ainsley arrived in the United States from England in 1884, and he arrived in Campbell two years later. After working as a farm hand in other orchards, he purchased his own land and began experimenting with canning fruit on a stove in his shed. In 1891, he produced the first 1,000 cases of canned fruit. By exporting the fruit to England (where Ainsley's brother supervised distribution), the J.C. Ainsley Packing Company became a huge success.

FOUR GENERATIONS OF AINSLEY WOMEN, 1920s. Pictured, from left to right, are Dorothy Ainsley Lloyd (J.C. Ainsley's daughter), Geraldine Lloyd Hicks (granddaughter), Alcinda Shelley Ainsley (wife), and Mrs. Mary C. Shelley.

J.C. Ainsley Packing Company Workers, 1893. By 1893, Ainsley had gone into partnership with his brother Dr. Thomas Ainsley, bought property adjacent to the railroad, and officially named his company the J.C. Ainsley Packing Company. Ainsley's canned fruit was very popular in England because of its quality.

Mikado Bartlett Pears, 1891. J.C. Ainsley selected "Mikado" for his first fruit label and had it patented in the United States and England. Ainsley wanted the name "Crown" but was informed that any name connected with royalty could not be used in England. Gilbert and Sullivan's *Mikado* was his favorite opera, so that became his first brand label.

AINSLEY PACKING CO. WORKERS. Ainsley is reputed to be the first to market fruit salad. It was marketed under the brand name "Golden Morn" and was called "Fruit Salad." It contained fruit that was too small to be canned separately. "Fruit Salad" contained larger pieces of this fruit, and "Fruit Cocktail" contained diced fruits.

AINSLEY PACKING CO. WORKERS. The packing plant was located on Harrison Street and Campbell Avenue. Group photographs of employees were taken every year.

AINSLEY PACKING CO. WORKERS. By 1929, the Ainsley Company had about 750 men and women on the payroll during peak season and produced about 300,000 cases of canned fruit. Production averaged from 5,000 to 6,000 tons of fruit each year, the bulk of it marketed in England. The Ainsley Cannery was the largest employer in Campbell and was well known for the consideration of its employees.

63

AINSLEY PACKING CO. WORKERS. The workers are eating lunch outside by the railroad tracks. Ainsley was the first employer to provide a nurse for his workers and supply a low-cost hot lunch. At the height of the fruit season, there was a shortage of housing in Campbell, and many people lived in tents. In 1912, for the convenience of his employees, Ainsley built cottages for them.

AINSLEY NURSERY PLAYGROUND, 1916. The J.C. Ainsley Packing Co. was one of the first canning companies to provide childcare and even kindergarten for its workers. Anna Banks Lloyd (seated) and her daughter Bernice Lloyd Soveker are looking after the children in the playground.

AINSLEY PACKING CO. WORKERS, 1911. These men were year-round workers for Ainsley, and the off-season provided a chance to expand with construction projects. Pictured here, from left to right, are Courtland L. Watson, Claude Gard, A. Brydon, Charlie DeSelle, and Tom Mendel.

THE AINSLEYS IN EGYPT, 1928. In this photograph, J.C. Ainsley and his wife, Alcinda, ride on top of camels during one of their many travels. The Campbell newspapers gave detailed accounts of the Ainsleys' European travels.

A WORLD WAR I SOLDIER'S LETTER. J.C. Ainsley received this Bluebell Brand Apricots label in the mail with the following letter written on the back:

Souvenir from the battlefield of Belgium Oct. 19, 1918. Perched high upon the end of a demolished British tank which had ended its career in a gigantic German shell hole. I rapaciously consumed the contents of this can of California peaches [sic]. For a brief moment I forgot Huns and battles as I licked the can clean. It sure was a rare and most palatable dish to one who had not tasted such a delicacy for months. Accept my profound thanks for the concern or individual who can grow and can such a luxury. Amid this scene of desolation, death and destruction it came like a gift from heaven. Sincerely yours, Cpl. Nelson G. Welburn Co. C" 316 Engrs. A.P.O. 776.

DREW CANNING COMPANY, C. 1935. The Old Settlers' Day Parade marches past the Drew Canning Company on Campbell Avenue. In 1933, J.C. Ainsley retired and sold his cannery to the Drew Canning Company.

HUNTS FOOD, 1940S. Drew sold the cannery to Hunts Food in 1946.

GEO. E. HYDE & CO. When grower support diminished for the Campbell Fruit Growers Union, George Hyde became the predominant stockholder. In 1909, he changed the name to Geo. E. Hyde & Company. Hyde continued to pack and dry fruit. By 1914, even though

Mr. Hyde had never canned before, over 1,000 tons of fruit had been canned or dried. He remained in business until 1929, when he sold the business to cannery workers.

MAUD HUSTED HYDE, 1909. Maud Husted married Ralph Henry Hyde, son of George E. Hyde, in 1909. In 1918, Ralph Hyde became president of the Campbell Water Company, and Maud Hyde served on the board of directors. Maud also served as president of the Water Company in 1938, a great achievement for a woman in those days.

GEO. E. HYDE & CO. The packinghouse was located on Central Avenue at the Southern Pacific tracks. The brick warehouse at the far left was built in 1894 by the Campbell Fruit Growers Union in an effort to minimize the financial losses incurred from their previously used low, wooden buildings where shrunken fruit was a result of inadequate storage.

DRYING YARD, 1917. This Geo. E. Hyde & Co. 17-acre drying yard ran along the railroad tracks and could hold almost 25,000 drying trays. Trays loaded with fruit were stacked on metal carts and wheeled along the rails through what became the largest drying yard in the world.

NURSERY. The cannery provided a playground for the children of the fruit workers at Geo E. Hyde & Co.

WAREHOUSE. This picture shows a Geo. E. Hyde & Co. warehouse, brimming with stacks of cans ready to be filled.

CANNING TABLES. During the height of the harvest season, these canning tables at Geo. E. Hyde & Co. would be filled with women peeling and cutting pears, peaches, apricots, and other fruits to fill the cans.

CANNING TABLES. This is a later view of the canning tables at Geo. E. Hyde & Co. with more machinery.

PEACH GRADERS AND CANNING TABLES ROOM. All the fruit had to be sorted or graded on quality. At Geo. E. Hyde & Co., a "fancy fruit" label was made with the biggest and best-quality fruits; the lowest quality went into a fruit cocktail.

SYRUPERS ROOM. After the fruit was put in the cans at Geo. E. Hyde & Co., these machines added the syrup.

CAN-CLOSING MACHINES. At Geo. E. Hyde & Co., once the syrup was added, these machines closed and sealed the cans. Then the cans were cooked to preserve the fruit inside.

LABELING MACHINE. Finally, with the fruit cooked inside the can, the can rolled on a conveyor belt to a labeling machine. The can would roll through glue and then roll over the label. Then the fruit was ready to be shipped out of the Geo. E. Hyde & Co. warehouse.

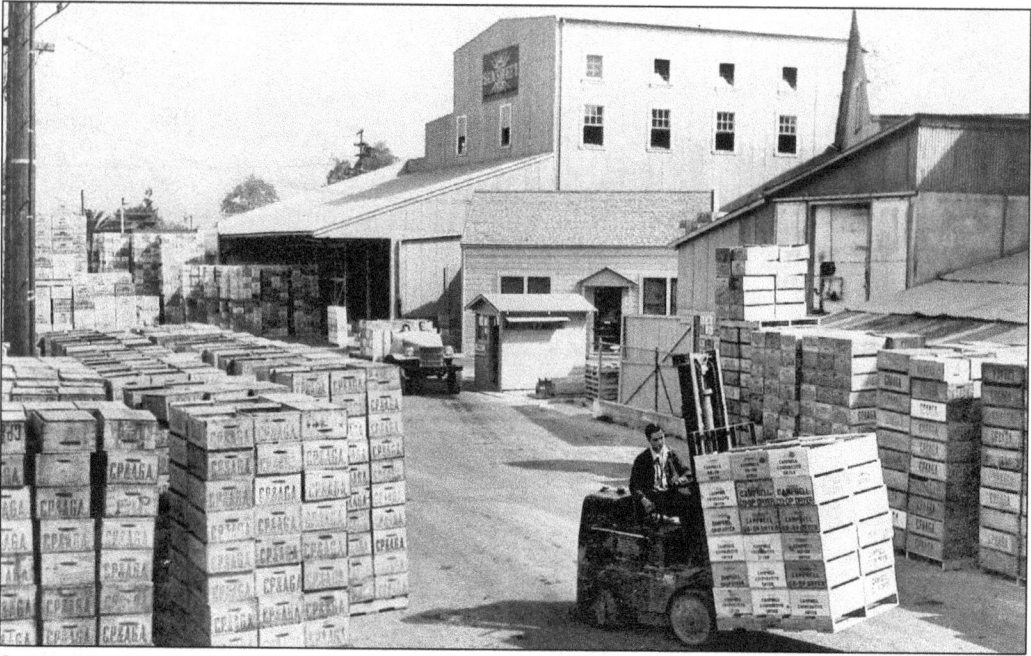

SUNSWEET PLANT 1. The California Prune and Apricot Growers Association began in 1917. In 1919, the association purchased the three-story building of the Farmers Union plant in Campbell, which became known as Sunsweet Plant 1. The Campbell–Los Gatos Prune and Apricot Association branched off in 1929.

SUNSWEET PLANT 1, 1930S. Growers of the association were expected to sign a marketing agreement, which accorded them one vote for each 10 tons of dried prunes and/or 5 tons of dried apricots they sorted. In this photograph, workers sort fruit underneath a dry shed. The first president of the board of directors for the Campbell–Los Gatos Prune and Apricot Association was Stanley B. Smith, founder of Orchard Supply Hardware.

PRUNES FOR CONSTIPATION

Prunes eaten regularly for breakfast exercise a natural and mild laxative effect in the alimentary canal that has given great relief to many sufferers from constipation. As a corrective agent in the diet and general system regulator they are unsurpassed by any other fruit.

If you have a tendency toward constipation, eat a generous dish of properly cooked Association Brand Prunes every morning, for several weeks. You'll be surprised at the difference it makes and how much better you will feel.

PRUNES IN CARTONS

The prunes in this package are selected from over eleven thousand California Orchards and are sold by the orchardists themselves through their cooperative organization.

Association Brand Cartons are packed in three sizes, 1 lb., 2 lb. and 5 lb. and the size of fruit contained is plainly marked in the panel on the face of the carton in different colors.

Grown and Packed
In the U. S. A.

NET CONTENTS 1 LB.

CALIFORNIA PRUNE
Sunsweet
TRADE MARK
AND APRICOT GROWERS ASS'N.

Association Brand

MEDIUM SIZE
FRUIT

California

PRUNES

CALIFORNIA PRUNE AND APRICOT GROWERS ASSOCIATION

Main Offices: SAN JOSE, CALIFORNIA

A Non-profit Co-operative Selling Organization
of over 11,375 Grower Members

Growers and Packers of the Famous Sunsweet
Red Label Cans and Cartons

Carton Made in U. S. A.

SUNSWEET. Courtesy of the California Prune and Apricot Growers Association, consumers could read the benefits of prunes for constipation along the side of the box.

SUNSWEET PLANT 1, PRUNE-SORTING MACHINE. Fruit from the association was marketed under the brand name of "Sunsweet," and people referred to the association as "Sunsweet." Each grower was required to weigh in their fruit on scales before unloading their labeled boxes at the dipper. The fruit was then dried at the Campbell Cooperative Dryer.

MEN CUTTING COTS FROM TRAYS. A group of about 50 growers formed the Campbell Co-op Dryer in 1937 with a plant that included four tunnels, a green fruit platform with a self-spreading dipper, and a 500-ton dry fruit warehouse. The co-op worked closely with the California Prune and Apricot Association. Growers had to belong to the association in order to have their fruit dried by the co-op.

SORTING FRUIT OFF THE CHUTE. In 1940, Campbell Co-op Dryer bought the Hyde drying yard. The co-op was advertised as the largest cooperative in the world and soon had the largest dehydrator in the world. After being dipped, each grower's prunes were put on trays and sent to tunnels, where they stayed for 16 hours at a temperature of 165 to 168 degrees.

MEN CHECKING THE GRADE OF FRUIT. After the fruit dried, workers scraped it off the drying trays into boxes, where it stayed for two weeks to "equalize." The fruit was then sent back to the association, or Sunsweet, next door, where it was placed on a huge grader and graded according to size. The association then made a record for the farmer since his payment would be based on the size of his fruit.

CARTON-MAKING MACHINE. This photograph shows a carton-making machine at Sunsweet Plant 1.

WOMEN PACKING FRUIT. The association owned the fruit once the farmer was paid, and all the fruit was stored together. The dried fruit was shipped to buyers from all over the world from this plant under the Sunsweet label.

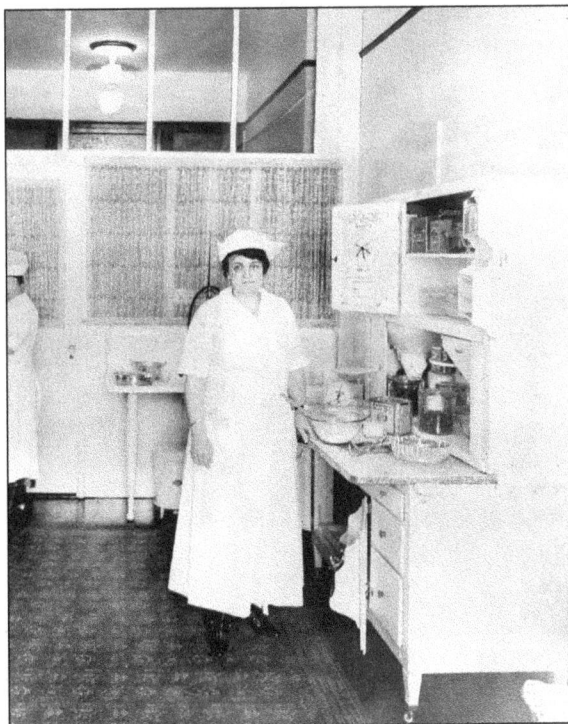

KITCHEN, 1930s. In this photograph, women work in the kitchens at Sunsweet.

SUNSWEET FLOAT, 1950s. Sunsweet boasted this float on Old Settlers' Day.

SUNSWEET WORKERS ON STRIKE, 1964. The Campbell Cooperative Dryer and the Campbell–Los Gatos Prune and Apricot Association ended in 1971 as orchards disappeared from Campbell and the surrounding area. The Sunsweet label, however, still exists today.

Five

EDUCATION

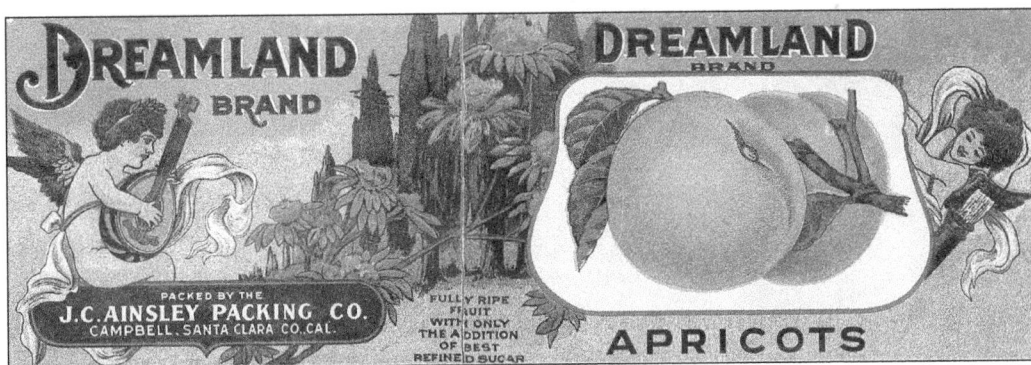

J.C. AINSLEY DREAMLAND BRAND APRICOTS. This label for Dreamland Brand Apricots is from 1900.

A CAMPBELL CLASSROOM, C. 1900. Education did not have high priority in the state legislature until 1855, when funding was provided for school districts. Districts were formed as the population increased with the continued arrival of pioneers.

MORELAND ELEMENTARY SCHOOL, C. 1895. The Moreland School District is the oldest rural school district still in operation in California. It began as a private school in 1851 with classes held in private homes. In 1852, Zechariah Moreland offered his home as a school for $250. S.C. Rogers, a teacher, visited families to collect money, and the district became official in 1853.

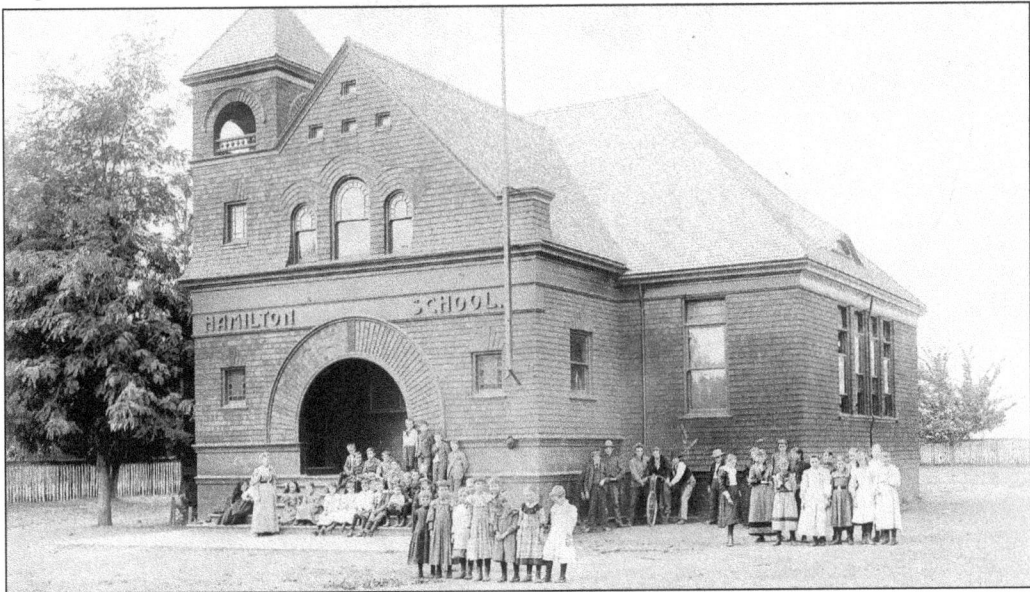

HAMILTON SCHOOL, C. 1910. The Hamilton School District, established in 1855, was named for Zeri and Jane Hamilton. The Hamiltons had nine children, and Mrs. Hamilton was the first teacher of Hamilton School. The first schoolhouse was probably their home or some other building on their property. Hamilton School District eventually combined with Campbell to create the Campbell Union School District.

CAMBRIAN ELEMENTARY SCHOOL CLASS, 1892. In 1863, the first Cambrian School was built on property donated by Lewis Casey, a pioneer of the Cambrian area. Casey came to the Santa Clara Valley in 1853 because he was told that the valley, unlike the mining towns of Sacramento, was settled with families.

SECOND CAMBRIAN SCHOOL, 1909. The old schoolhouse was later replaced with a two-room building situated on the same site. The Cambrian District got its name from David Lewis, a farm hand on the Casey ranch, who was instrumental in providing funds for building the school. He suggested naming the school after his homeland, Cambria, which is Latin for Wales.

UNION SCHOOL. Union School was established in 1863 by local ranchers who sympathized with the Union cause in the Civil War. The teacher for the school lived in the homes of the children, staying a few weeks with each. This school building was erected in 1914.

MERIDIAN SCHOOL, 1926. Meridian School District formed in 1897. The schoolhouse was dedicated in 1904, and two teachers were responsible for four grades each. In 1920, Meridian School District merged with Campbell.

CAMPBELL GRAMMAR SCHOOL, 1896. The Campbell School District started in 1888, and the second schoolhouse was built in 1896. The building housed the Campbell Grammar School, and in 1900 (when Campbell High School started), the first classes were held on the second floor until a separate high school was built.

CAMPBELL GRAMMAR SCHOOL, C. 1910. This photograph shows a view of Campbell Grammar School from next door at Campbell High School.

PRES. THEODORE ROOSEVELT, 1903. Pictured at center are, from left to right, President Roosevelt (wearing a top hat and holding a shovel), J. Fred Smith, and Benjamin Campbell. The president was invited to Campbell in a letter from J. Fred Smith. Smith moved to Campbell from Iowa in 1899 to become the high school's founding principal. In 1900, a bond issue passed to form the Campbell Union High School District; however, most district residents did not see the need for a separate high school building. In 1903, Pres. Theodore Roosevelt was planning a visit to San Jose. Smith believed that if Roosevelt came to Campbell and planted a tree on the proposed high school grounds, the community would be more open to building a separate high school facility by the tree.

PRES. THEODORE ROOSEVELT'S ENTOURAGE, 1903. In this photograph, Roosevelt's entourage parades down Campbell Avenue during his memorable visit. Later, in the Campbell High School yearbook, an account of Roosevelt's visit read as follows:

> Campbell enjoyed a peculiar distinction among the high schools of the State during President Roosevelt's visit to the coast. During his ride through this valley he stopped at Campbell to plant a tree in the name of the high school. Mr. Roosevelt turned to the children and said: ". . . I want to see you play hard while you play and when you work do not play at all."

CAMPBELL UNION HIGH SCHOOL, C. 1910. The high school was built in 1904, after Roosevelt's tree-planting visit, on the corner of Campbell Avenue and present-day Winchester Boulevard. Note the Roosevelt Coastal Redwood tree on the right. The building had separate entrances for boys and girls.

90

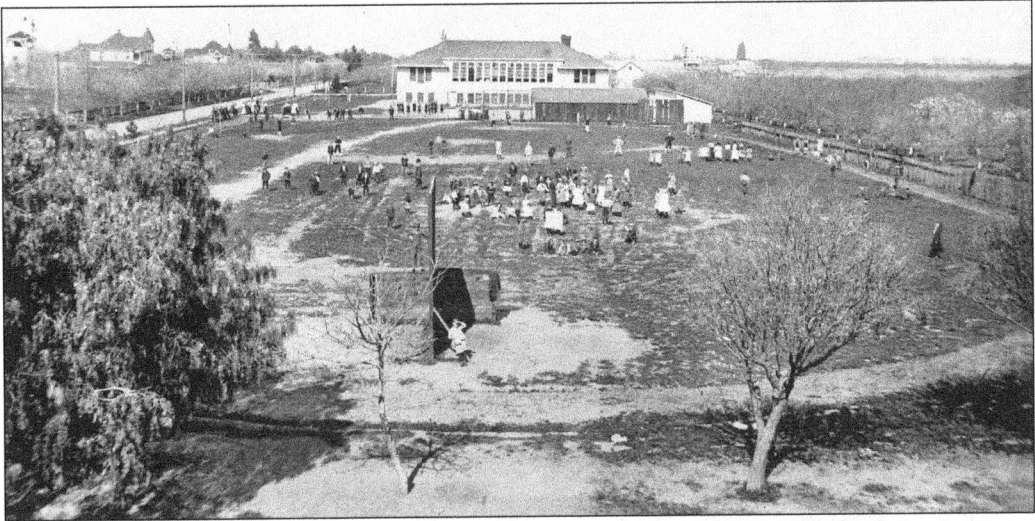

CAMPBELL UNION HIGH SCHOOL, C. 1910. Another view from the back of the high school was taken from Campbell Grammar School. A horse shed out back provided stalls for the students' transportation. Present-day downtown Campbell can be seen to the distant left with nothing else around except for fields.

GIRLS BASKETBALL TEAM, 1903. The girls at Campbell Union High School had a basketball team before the boys did. Pictured, from left to right, are the following: (front row) Mabel Ross, Nina Davidson, and Alice Joy; (middle row) ? Fablinger, Maude Farley, Della Kennison, and Ellen Walpeman; (back row) C. Foster, Fran Fablinger, and Anna B. Ross.

TRACK TEAM, 1904. Members of the Campbell Union High School track team are pictured here, from left to right, as follows: (front row) unidentified and Clyde Betts; (middle row) Thaddeus Joy, John Lonard, and Albert Cragin; (back row) George Schuyler and F.L. Righter.

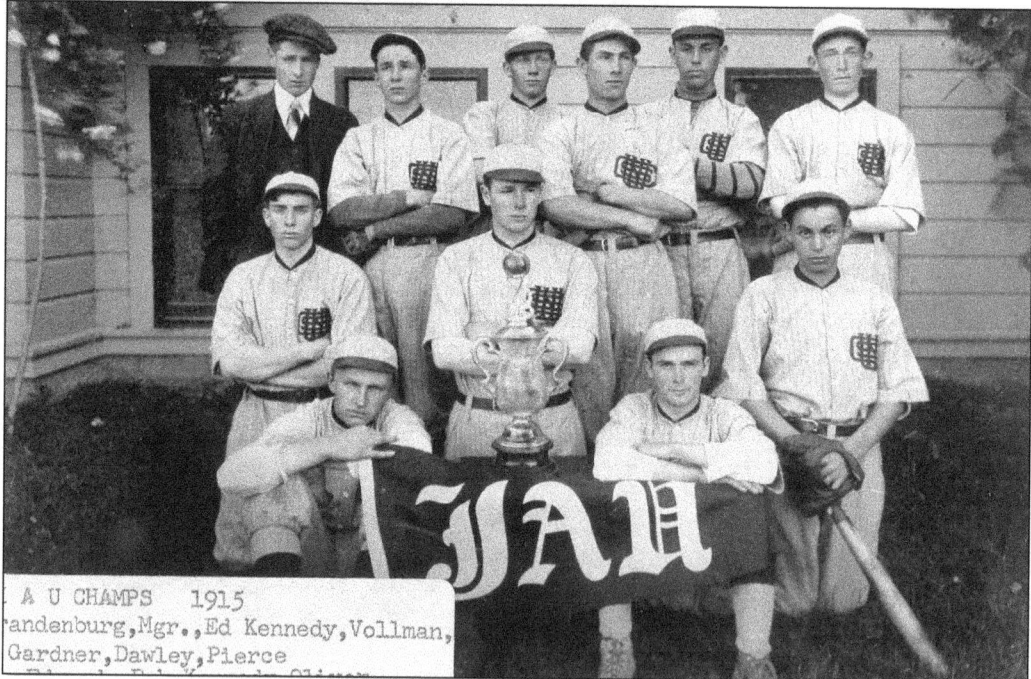

A U CHAMPS 1915
andenburg,Mgr.,Ed Kennedy,Vollman,
Gardner,Dawley,Pierce

BASEBALL CHAMPIONS, 1915. The Campbell Union High School baseball team and the winners of the IAU Championship included the following: ? Brandenburg (manager), Ed Kennedy, ? Vollman, ? Gardner, ? Dawley, Pierce Edwards, Bob Kennedy, Oliver Righter, and Pat Kennedy.

TRACK TEAM, 1920. The Campbell Union High School track team poses here. From left to right are Elmer Hoerler, Raymond Hulseman, Al Gross, Fred Heinzen, George Benner, Emil Mrak, and D.H. Cramer (coach). Cramer became the third principal and superintendent of Campbell Union High School in 1920.

CAMPBELL UNION HIGH SCHOOL PLAY, 1926. The high school seniors performed *Sherwood* in 1926. Lillian Gard Maloney (seated) played Queen Elinor, and Patricia Hunter Harding (standing) performed Marian.

THE NEW CAMPBELL UNION HIGH SCHOOL, JUNE 1938. In 1936, enrollment at Campbell High School passed the 500 mark, and it became clear that Campbell needed a larger school. Architect William H. Weeks designed the new high school building. Students, faculty, parents, and community leaders attended the laying of the cornerstone for the auditorium, as seen in the left foreground of this photograph. Workers constructed the school over a two-year period, from 1936 to 1938.

CAMPBELL UNION HIGH SCHOOL, 1940s. This photograph shows the completed high school from the corner of Campbell Avenue and Winchester Boulevard. In 1980, Campbell High School closed due to a decline in enrollment. Now the historic building serves as the Campbell Community Center. The old high school auditorium was reopened as the Heritage Theatre in 2004.

READY TO GO. The Campbell Union High School band is pictured here in 1937.

BOWS AND STRINGS. The Campbell Union High School string orchestra poses in 1950.

HIGH SCHOOL FOOTBALL, 1944. The Campbell Buccaneers played on a dirt field between orchards until all the other schools refused to play at Campbell unless it had a grass field. In 1938, Campbell Union High School planted a grass football field.

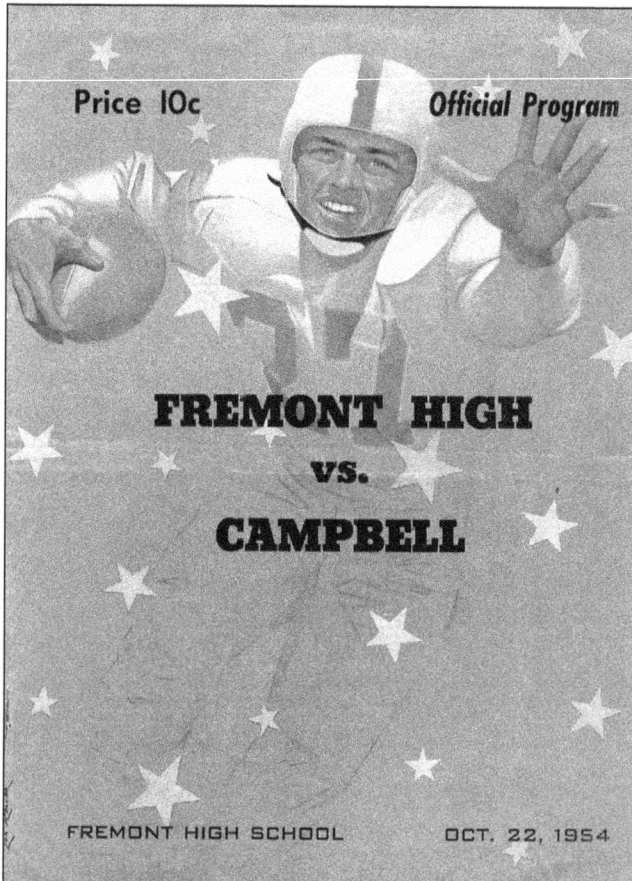

Price 10c   Official Program

FREMONT HIGH

vs.

CAMPBELL

FREMONT HIGH SCHOOL   OCT. 22, 1954

FREMONT HIGH VS. CAMPBELL, 1954. Shown is a program from a game between Fremont High and Campbell Union High.

Six

COMMUNITY LIFE

SUNSWEET CALIFORNIA PRUNES.
The date of this Sunsweet
California Prunes label is unknown.

CAMPBELL AVENUE, LOOKING EAST, C. 1910. On the right side of the street are the Odd Fellows Hall, the Peter Arnott residence (with palm trees), and the Al Smith Auto Shop. A fire wiped out the entire block between the Odd Fellows Hall and the Bank of Campbell around 1913. The bank building had not yet been conceived when this picture was taken.

DOWNTOWN CAMPBELL AVENUE, 1930S. In this photograph taken from the Southern Pacific tracks, Campbell's first movie theater, the Campbell Theatre, is visible on the left.

DOWNTOWN CAMPBELL AVENUE, 1940S. This photograph was taken from the same vantage point of the downtown area (the Southern Pacific tracks) only a decade later.

CALIFORNIA LADIES BAND, C. 1900. Music was an important form of community entertainment. Often, traveling bands would perform at Campbell Hall, which was built for town meetings and social functions.

SAN JOSE PARADE, C. 1900. This photograph shows Campbell's first float in a San Jose parade.

CAMPBELL BANNER, 1917. The San Jose parade was in celebration of Liberty Loan Day in October 1917.

"HEART OF THE VALLEY" FLOAT, C. 1930. This float appeared in the Old Settlers' Day Parade, shown here passing the Ainsley House on the corner of Bascom and Hamilton Avenues. Old Settlers' Day began on July 4, 1892, when the community met at the new Campbell Fruit Growers Union facility for a flag raising and picnic lunch.

Sunsweet Float, 1956. By 1895, the Old Settlers' Day program was moved to Washington's Birthday in February probably because farmers were busy in July with their harvest. An official parade became part of the program in 1939, and Sunsweet Association usually submitted a float.

Mrs. Jessie Campbell, 1951. Jessie McKenzie Campbell was the widow of James H. Campbell and was Benjamin Campbell's only daughter-in-law. She was given "Queen" status over Old Settlers' Day for many years until her death.

CAMPBELL KIWANIS-MASONIC QUARTET, 1926. The quartet was composed of community leaders. Pictured here, from left to right, are Dr. Walter I. Merrill, who sang bass; Herold Morton, a lumberman whose son became Campbell's first mayor, baritone; Harold Cramer, high school principal and teacher, tenor; and Harry C. Smith, newspaper editor and postmaster, tenor.

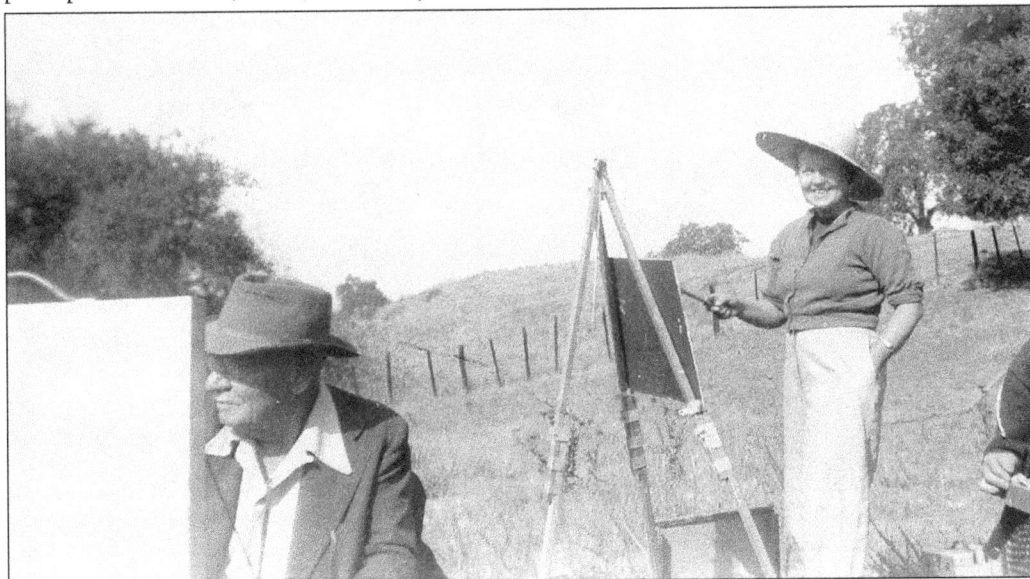

FRANK H. CUTTING, C. 1960. Frank Cutting (on the left) was a teacher, orchardist, and Campbell's most famous landscape artist. In 1917, after receiving an inheritance, Cutting devoted himself full-time to painting. His paintings have been exhibited at Stanford University, San Jose State University, the Palace of the Legion of Honor, and various art galleries. His gallery was located on Harrison Avenue.

PUNDITA CIRCLE. The Pundita Circle was organized in 1908 by a group of 11 women who joined to form a reading club. The name of the club was in honor of Pundita Ramabai, one of India's most educated women of that era. Pundita means "learned women," and the purpose of the club was to improve the women's knowledge by studying various topics.

COUNTRY WOMAN'S CLUB, C. 1950. Pictured here at this past presidents luncheon are, from left to right, Ida Price, Millie Eliza Jeffers, L.J. Carboni, Mrs. Roberta J. Field, Mrs. Etta Allison, Mrs. Maude Hyde, and Mrs. Sylvia Jacobsen. The Country Woman's Club was officially chartered in 1905. The purpose of the club was to "increase kindly fellowship; to encourage high thought and free speech upon all matters of general interest; to foster worthy talent in our midst; and to aid the growth of the Campbell Free Library." Later, the focus was enlarged to include community and educational projects involving, for example, the museum, seniors, parks and recreation, and high school scholarships. The club continues to focus on educational projects today.

COUNTRY WOMAN'S CLUB MEMBERS, 1920S. This photograph shows club members fund-raising to help build a new library. The first project the club undertook was to create the Campbell Free Library. Once incorporated, the women immediately paid to rent a room for the library in the Sutter Building.

FIRST CAMPBELL PUBLIC LIBRARY, 1907. The Country Woman's Club raised enough money to purchase Benjamin Campbell's lot and construct a small wooden building on the corner of First and Campbell Avenues. The *Campbell Interurban Press* praised their actions, saying, "Hurrah for the women and the Library."

FANNY JANES MERRILL, 1897. Fanny Janes Merrill was a founding member of the Country Woman's Club. Her father, Prof. Elijah Janes, worked with the Campbell YMCA to start the first collection of books for the library. He also served, without compensation, as Campbell's first librarian until his death in 1917.

MARY LEWIS, C. 1920. In this photograph, Mary Lewis, Campbell's second librarian, sits in front of Campbell's first library. Confined to a wheelchair for most of her life, she served as Campbell's librarian from 1917 to 1923. The Country Woman's Club helped pay her salary.

LIBRARY ON CAMPBELL AVENUE, 1923. The Country Woman's Club worked hard to raise the funds for this building, which was constructed in 1923. It was the second library that was built by the club. The library occupied the room to the right of the front steps, and the clubroom to the left was available for community events.

THE FOOTLIGHTERS IN *THE CITY SLICKER*, 1950. For over 15 years, Campbell enjoyed a community theater group called the Footlighters. Their first production, *Aron Slick from Pumpkin Crik*, debuted in 1940.

CARRIE WATSON WITH HER BICYCLE, C. 1900. In 1896, Susan B. Anthony said, "The bicycle has done more for the emancipation of women than anything else in the world."

WILLIAM JENNINGS BRYAN, C. 1900. A Sunday drive and picnic was a favorite pastime. Since picnics were often on Sundays, everyone wore their finest clothes.

GRAB A RACKET. These tennis players pose for a 1920 photograph.

THE SIGHTS OF FALL. These well-dressed folks pose in a pumpkin patch in Campbell *c.* 1900.

AERIAL VIEW OF CAMPBELL, 1960S. Campbell is still called the "Orchard City" because for many years the small downtown area was surrounded with orchards. By 1935, there were 120,000 acres of prunes growing in "the Valley of Heart's Delight." This view of Campbell, including Highway 17 and Campbell Avenue, illustrates the shift from a rural community to a city in the heart of Silicon Valley.

Seven

LANDMARKS

OF CAMPBELL

J.C. AINSLEY FOREST KING FRUIT SALAD. This label dates from *c.* 1920.

CAMPBELL WATER TANK, C. 1912. In 1892, the Campbell Water Company provided water for Campbell. The first tank fell in the 1906 earthquake. These are the four wooden stave tanks that piped water into town. The rate in 1909 for a family of five was $1 per month.

AERIAL VIEW OF CAMPBELL. This picture captures the view from the top of the 1898 grammar school site before it was demolished in 1917. Benjamin Campbell's windmill is in the foreground, and the central building is the 1916 Mission Hatchery.

CAMPBELL WATER TOWER, 2004. In 1975, the Campbell Water Company merged with the San Jose Water Company; however, the Campbell water tower remains a landmark in the city.

CAMPBELL FIRE STATION NO. 1 AND FIRST CITY HALL, 1961. Campbell became incorporated in 1952. The fire station, built at 51 North Central Avenue, became the first building owned by the new city. From 1952 to 1957, the building served as the fire station, police station, and city offices. The fire engines occupied the front of the building, and the police and city clerk shared an office. The city clerk, Dorothy Trevethan, had three phones on her desk: one for the fire department, one for the police department, and one for city business. Now the old fire station houses the Campbell Historical Museum.

CAMPBELL'S SECOND CITY HALL, 1957–1971. The second city hall was located in the former Congressional church, built in 1893.

CAMPBELL CITY HALL AND CLOCK TOWER, 1971. Today's Campbell City Hall was finished in 1971. The complex, designed by William Hedley Jr., included the Campbell Library opposite city hall. The clock tower was built with citizen donations. Concealed in the base of the tower is a time capsule, from the citizens of 1971, to be opened by the citizens of 2071.

FIRST CITY COUNCIL MEETING, JULY 1971. Inside the new council chambers are, from left to right, council members William Smeed, Ed Rogers, Ralph Doetch, William R. Podgorsek, and Dean Chamberlain.

115

CAMPBELL PUBLIC LIBRARY UNDER CONSTRUCTION, 1974. This photograph shows the Campbell Library in its current location.

LOS GATOS CREEK TRAIL AND PAR COURSE, 1990. In 1973, the Los Gatos Creek Linear Park Recreation Project began with the City of Campbell working alongside the County Parks and Recreation Department and Commission, the Town of Los Gatos, and the County Flood Control District. The Pruneyard towers are in the distance.

CAMPBELL POLICE DEPARTMENT, 1958. Shown here, from left to right, are the following: (front row) John Morgan (future chief and youngest chief in California), Robert Locke (chief), and Gordon Rooney; (back row) Clyde Harris, Carl Arnold, Louis Wilson, and Don Burr (future chief). The first issue of the *Campbell Weekly Visitor* in 1895 stated, "Mr. B. Campbell is now a full-fledged Justice of the Peace. He will be in his office on Campbell Avenue ready for business in a short time." Campbell continued to have a justice of the peace until the city became incorporated in 1952.

FEMALE MEMBERS, CAMPBELL POLICE DEPARTMENT, 1974. Campbell's first woman police officer, Donna Perry (far right), was hired in 1974. The police department officially began after Campbell became incorporated. With two officers, one officer patrolled at night, the other officer during the day. The first ticket, remembers one early officer, was issued to a Campbell "hot rodder."

VOLUNTEER FIRE DEPARTMENT'S FIRST TRUCK. The 1913 Model T American LaFrance came equipped with 2 chemical tanks, a 12-foot ladder, 2 oil lanterns, 2 axes, and 50 feet of 1-inch rubber hose. It cost $1,775 and served until 1937. The original fire station stands in the background; it was located on the east side of Campbell Avenue between Campbell and Hyde Cannery.

CAMPBELL VOLUNTEER FIRE DEPARTMENT, 1926. The Campbell Volunteer Fire Department, shown here in front of the Curry Building, became official in 1912. Volunteers purchased their own badges at $1 apiece, and the following equipment was purchased: 200 feet of 2-inch cotton hose, a water cart, galvanized iron pails, and 2 ladders. Apparently, keeping track of ladders was a problem. An ad placed in the newspaper in 1900 urged "all parties to leave ladders belonging to fire dept. in their places." An addendum later added "except in case of fire."

ED GENASCI. Campbell Volunteer Fire Chief Ed Genasci served as the second fire chief (1919–1941). At the start of World War II, he left for a military camp in San Luis Obispo. As many volunteers were inducted into military service, the volunteer fire department had to recruit high school boys and older men.

JACK B. SCOTT, 1940s. Jack Scott was the third chief of the volunteer fire department and held that position from 1941 to 1952. When Campbell incorporated in 1952, Scott became the first official fire chief of the City of Campbell's fire department. He was not provided with a salary but was given a "reasonable expense account."

CAMPBELL VOLUNTEER FIREMAN. The bills on the back of firefighters' helmets helped protect their necks and kept debris from falling down the back of their coats. Before protective face gear was used, firefighters turned their helmets around to protect their faces from the heat.

120

CAMPBELL'S FIRST PARAMEDIC CREW, 1970S. Pictured here, from left to right, are the following: (front row) Mike Johnson, Rick Kinkaid, George Renshaw, and Ray Ravero; (back row) Gary Salmon, Al Lowder, Fred Van Hook, and Fred Bailey. In 1974, the Campbell Fire Department gained statewide attention when it started the first paramedic program in Northern California. A new TV series at the time, *Emergency*, which was about paramedics in Southern California, brought public attention to emergency mobile medical response teams for the first time. The city's goals committee recommended that the city council start a program similar to those in Los Angeles. After a year of training at their own expense, eight men became certified paramedics. With a 1974 Chevrolet truck outfitted with compartments for a portable EKG, suction, a hospital radio, expanded medical kits, and the Hurst rescue tool, the paramedic Rescue Squad 25 was officially in service.

CAMPBELL FIRE-PREVENTION AWARD, 1968. Gov. Ronald Reagan presents a fire-prevention award to Campbell Fire Chief George Maxwell. From left to right are Bill Smeed, representing the city council; Chief Maxwell; Senator Alquist; Governor Reagan; and Al LaPlante and Ken Mantle of the Campbell Chamber of Commerce. Chief Maxwell created a fire-prevention program to educate schoolchildren about fire safety. In 1967, the city got national recognition when the National Fire Protection Association ranked Campbell's fire department first place in the United States. Campbell also received first place in the state of California in 1967, 1968, and 1969.

FIRE IN CAMPBELL, 1990S. Throughout the 1970s and 1980s, the city grew rapidly. Several times, joining forces with the Central Fire District seemed a viable option. Finally, in 1993, the Campbell Fire Department became a part of the larger Santa Clara County Fire District.

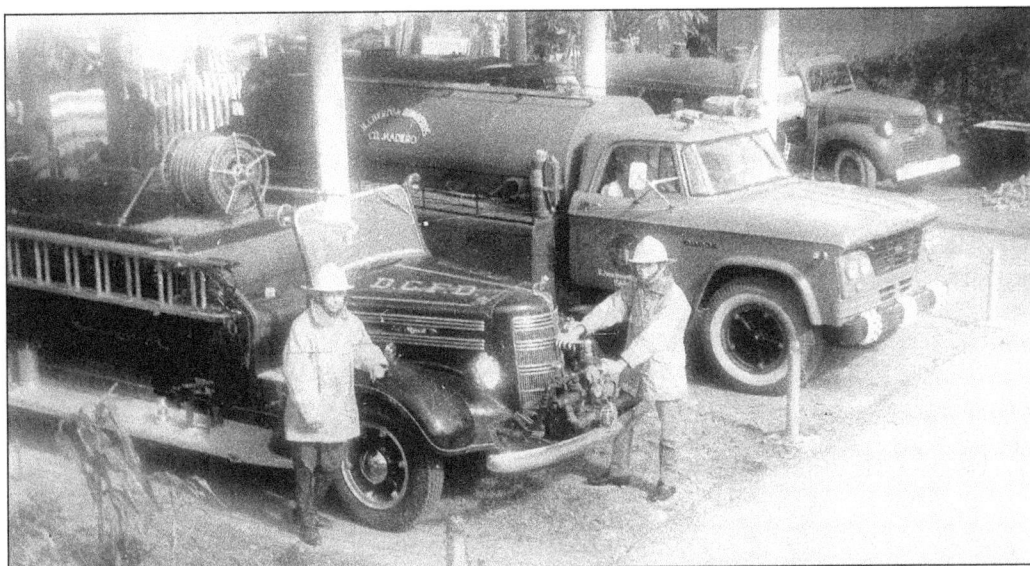

CAMPBELL FIRE DEPARTMENT'S SISTER CITY, MADERO, 1968. The Campbell Fire Department created a partnership with Madero, Mexico, by which older equipment and gear was donated to Madero, where adequate funds to support their firefighters were lacking.

CAMPBELL FIRE STATION NO. 2, C. 1965. The Sunnyoaks Station opened in 1969 after eight years of using this converted residence at 776 Sunnyoaks Avenue. A training tower, which is still in use today, was also built on the grounds of the new station. Union Avenue Station was then built in 1982. To get downstairs to the fire engines in a hurry, Union Station firefighters used slides instead of poles. Slides are safer than poles because there is less risk of injury on the way down.

DOWNTOWN CAMPBELL AVENUE, 1979. The historic 1895 bank building is now an architect's office. The two-story Downing Building with the curved façade is visible in the middle of the block on the left side, and the 1911 Curry Building with the peaked tower stands just beyond it.

HERITAGE THEATRE, C. 1940. The original 1938 Campbell Union High School auditorium had been in disrepair since the school closed in 1980. After being restored as a community theater, the auditorium opened as the Heritage Theatre in 2004.

AINSLEY HOUSE. This English Tudor Revival house, built in 1925 and pictured here in its original location in 1948, was the Ainsleys' retirement home. The house and its furnishings are a wonderful example of the Arts and Crafts movement of the 1920s. In 1989, the granddaughters of J.C. Ainsley, Geraldine Hicks, and Georgene Bowen donated the house and its contents to the City of Campbell. The house was moved to its present location at 300 Grant Street in 1990. Today the house is operated as a museum and is open for tours.

JEANETTE WATSON. Former curator and first woman mayor of Campbell, Jeanette Watson was instrumental in organizing the Campbell Historical Museum & Ainsley House and making it a professional organization. Her book *Campbell, the Orchard City* is the most complete book on Campbell history to date.

"APRICOTS AND PRUNES," 2000. The Campbell Historical Museum features innovative exhibits with hands-on sections where visitors can handle objects, allowing them to connect with days gone by. These exhibits are not specific only to Campbell history; rather, they focus on common cultural themes such as home, recreation, work, and community.

Watercolor illustration
by Marjorie K. Shull, ©2003

CAMPBELL HISTORICAL MUSEUM. After the Campbell Fire Department no longer used Station No. 1, the Campbell Historical Museum moved to the building in 1983. The museum officially opened in 1964; however, a permanent home was elusive until the old fire station was designated for the museum. Now both the Campbell Historical Museum and the Ainsley House are open to the public and for educational tours.

CELEBRATING THE BEST OF AMERICA IN CAMPBELL, 2004. Janine Sato, a fifth-grader from Castlemont Elementary School, was the first-place winner in a poster contest sponsored by the Civic Improvement Commission. She writes:

> On my poster I drew several things that represent the best of Campbell in America. I drew the Campbell water tower, the Ainsley House, the Historical Museum, the Sunsweet logo, the first Campbell Union High school bus, the city of Campbell emblem, and books to represent the Campbell Library. The water tower, the Ainsley House and the Historical Museum are all landmarks in Campbell and represent Campbell's history. The Sunsweet logo and the emblem shows that Campbell was an orchard city that grew a lot of prunes and apricots through the Sunsweet growers association. Finally, the Campbell High School bus represents the youth of Campbell and that it's part of Campbell's history too.

www.ingramcontent.com/pod-product-compliance
Lightning Source LLC
Chambersburg PA
CBHW080605110426
42813CB00006B/1415